Write It on Your Heart

Other books by Carolyn Sutton:
  Eye-openers
  Journey to Joy
  No More Broken Places
  Staying Vertical

To order, call 1-800-765-6955.
  Visit us at www.reviewandherald.com for information
on other Review and Herald® products.

Write It On Your Heart

HOW TO MAKE JOURNALING WORK FOR YOU

Carolyn Sutton

WITH LUCILE ROTH

rR

REVIEW AND HERALD® PUBLISHING ASSOCIATION
HAGERSTOWN, MD 21740

The author assumes full responsibility for the accuracy of all facts and quotations as cited in this book.

This book was
Edited by Delma Miller
Designed by Freshcut Design
Cover photo by Getty Images/The Image Bank/Tim Bieber
Typeset: 11/14 Bembo

PRINTED IN U.S.A.

08 07 06 05 04   5 4 3 2 1

R&H Cataloging Service
Sutton, Carolyn, 1944-
    Write it on your heart: how to make journaling work for you,
by Carolyn Sutton and Lucile Roth.

    1. Diaries—Authorship—Religious aspects.   2. Spiritual journals.
I. Roth, Lucile.   II. Title.

248

ISBN 0-8280-1820-0

Dedication

I lovingly dedicate this book
to the memory
of my most unflagging supporter and husband,

LaVerne W. Roth, Sr.

At the beginning he helped on his computer,
and always believed we would finish this project.
—Lucile

I lovingly dedicate this book
to the memory
of my first writing instructor and mother,

Lucile Roth

She fell asleep in Jesus
two days after we finished this project.
We'll resume our collaboration . . . in the morning.
—Carolyn

Contents

WHY JOURNAL?

"Write this for a memorial in a book" (Ex. 17:14).

While helping my mother move a while back, I ran across a dusty packet. Cobweb-coated, it lay in the bottom of a partially disintegrated cardboard box she hadn't opened in years.

Wiping off the cobwebs with a rag, I carefully unclasped the packet. Amazed, I discovered a sizable stack of letters that *I* had written 30 years ago!

Encapsulated in these hastily penned missives were spontaneous and endearing vignettes about my son from the age of 18 to 25 months. What a treasured find!

And my mother—who loves writing, correspondence, and journaling—had saved them!

With nearly insatiable interest, intermittent laughter, and nostalgic tears I relived little Kent's precious antics. Once again I thrilled at early evidence of his delightful first love for Jesus.

Never would I have remembered these precious moments had I not written them down.

The contents of these letters also reminded me how supportive my extended family had been during a difficult and uncertain time in my life.

Ah, and the friends who had quietly slipped in and out between the lines . . . How could I ever have forgotten their kindnesses? Yet, I *had* forgotten. Those letters, however, helped me recall just how much we had weathered together—the milestones we'd celebrated, the losses we'd grieved. The reawakening of old memories flooded my heart with warmth for people I hadn't thought about in a long, long time. Suddenly I realized that all these remembered blessings and earlier friendships would have been lost to me had I not written about them.

In the intervening years I'd also forgotten about someone else. That someone else was *me*—who I was back then compared to who I am today.

WRITING TO REMEMBER

Though I've saved very few letters during the years, I have developed the habit of corresponding with another Friend—God. I've done this through a variety of journals. As with rereading my old letters, rereading these journals awakens lost memories of His goodness, comfort, strength, and power working on my behalf. Rereading these personal chronicles of His love helps me get over current jarring bumps in life's road.

Throughout Bible times God instructed certain individuals to keep personal journals. He told Moses, "Write this for a memorial in a book" (Ex. 17:14). "Be sure to get it down on papyrus, Moses, so you won't forget everything we've come through together!" Much of the Pentateuch is a travel journal kept by Moses during the children of Israel's desert sojourn.

David recorded events, thoughts, and feelings during

much of his lifetime, as well. In fact, he referred to himself as "a ready writer" penning his emotional prayers to God (Ps. 45:1).

Even God got in on writing so that we would remember. In fact, He Himself wrote the Ten Commandments with His own finger (Ex. 31:18; 32:16).

Samuel, Nathan, and Gad recorded events during the reign of King David (1 Chron. 29:29).

Chroniclers of King Hezekiah recorded in official books the highlights of his rule (2 Kings 20:20).

Once Elijah journaled about a wicked king's actions (King Libnah) and then commented on the consequences of those actions before sending the journal to the king himself (2 Chron. 21:12)!

Ezra the scribe (Ezra 7:6, 11; Neh. 8:1) and head contractor Nehemiah kept detailed records of what took place before, during, and after the rebuilding of Jerusalem's broken wall.

In Esther's day, King Ahasuerus's court recorders kept a journal of people and events that helped protect and perpetuate his reign (Esther 6:1, 2).

In New Testament times, the apostle Paul reminded the Corinthians that events of the past had been recorded in writing to help posterity remember and learn (1 Cor. 10:11).

God uses the metaphor of recording-to-remember in a number of places. He even asked the Israelites to write, read, remember, and share about His leading in their history (Deut. 6:8; 11:18). Likewise, God instructs us to write His words and commandments upon "the tablet of your heart" (Prov. 7:3, NKJV).

My favorite writing-related text in Scripture, however, is Christ's promise to write "the name of my God" upon every person who overcomes through Him (Rev. 3:12).

CONFESSIONS OF AN UNFAITHFUL JOURNAL KEEPER

I used to think that to be a true journal keeper, I had to consistently write each day. An equal erroneous notion I held was that only a few types of journal styles exist and I must keep within their confines.

However, my own wandering, intermittent writing patterns have taught me otherwise, bringing me to this happy conclusion. I don't have to be a slave to someone else's writing style. *I* am in charge of my journal. My journal is *not* in charge of me. Therefore, I don't have to be consistent in my writing. I can customize my journal (or concurrent journals) according to the twists and turns of my personal journey.

For extended periods I've had neither the desire nor the felt need to journal. At other times—and by God's design, I believe—sporadic journaling has played a crucial and extremely positive role in both my life and the lives of others. I believe journaling can do the same for you.

When journaling meets our particular needs, it not only enables a closer intimacy with God but also provides some fabulous possibilities for friendship and encouragement ministries.

Here are just a few of the benefits journaling could hold for you.

- Journaling enables one to take the time to interact more thoughtfully with God.
- Journaling dissects both the happy and unhappy

stresses of life, bringing greater understanding of one's personal journey.

- Journaling helps one cope with periods of unexpected transition. (Often, seeing a tough situation written down on paper makes it seem more manageable.)
- Journaling fosters creativity. (It jump-starts the mind.)
- Journaling leads to exciting projects down the road—for many people—that can greatly benefit others.

Write It on Your Heart, the book you're holding in your hands, is really two books in one. First, it is an easy-to-read minicourse on how to journal—in other words, a handbook. It provides quick examples and an overview of 15 different journaling methods (not an exhaustive list, by any means).

Second, this book, by the time you complete it, will be your own personalized journal "sampler." It will be full of your own writing samples. (And who knows? Maybe you are adept at a writing style you never thought possible!)

At the end of each chapter are suggestions to help you find and develop your own customized journaling style. Subsequent journals can become ongoing "companions," that reflect your personality, needs, and journey for particular seasons of your life. *Write It on Your Heart* also brims with Bible study pointers for how to make your spiritual walk more practical and rewarding.

NUTS AND BOLTS OF JOURNALING

In one of my seminars someone once asked, "What do

I need in order to start journaling?"

First of all, your journal can be as simple as the back of an envelope or just a lined yellow notepad. That's how a couple of my mother's and mine started out.

At the other end of the spectrum, of course, some journal keepers do all their writing on a computer. I sort of mix and match. My Memorization Journal is on my computer. My Blessings Journal and a Subjects-of-Need Journal, however, I write by hand, as they are both part of my personal devotionals.

My "Journalistic" Journal—not directly related to my morning devotional time—I keep in a file on my laptop. Mother, my collaborator on this book, is now legally blind. So she dictates to me anything she wants written down.

Do whatever works for you—but do *something!*

Two women's Bible study leaders I know—in two different towns—both strongly recommend that their members journal in *some* way. In fact, one of these generous women feels so strongly about journaling that she recently purchased, at a local discount store, an inexpensive—but colorful—hardback book for each of us in her group (now we have no excuse *not* to journal)!

Some people don't journal because they aren't sure how to start. If you are one of these individuals, think of journaling as making plans to go shopping with a girlfriend (how hard is that?). When I have a date to meet a girlfriend for lunch or shopping, I plan ahead, usually the evening before.

I repack my purse, making sure I've included my planner, checkbook, any necessary credit or shopping club cards, a comb, and gloves—if the weather's going to be cold. I plan ahead because I want our together time the following day to be a carefree and enjoyable rendezvous. I always anticipate our get-togethers with a sense of freedom and adventure.

Our girlfriend times are never ritualistic. Journaling doesn't have to be either. As with my shopping trip preparations, so it is with my journaling preparation.

Since I'm *not* a morning person (when I get out of bed, anyway), I need to have planned ahead. The night before, I lay out the following within arm's reach of my old, overstuffed "devotional" chair (though these materials may change as my needs do).

- A Bible (or Bibles for comparative purposes)
- A journal (or journals) and at least two pens with different colored ink
- Highlighters for marking Bible passages or journal thoughts
- A list of current memorization goals
- Any auxiliary books I also plan to read
- Stickies (for thoughts I don't want to forget; Scripture references I want to study later; texts that might encourage someone currently going through tough stuff)
- The day's to-do list (as a depository for intruding mental traffic—I can jot down quick reminders for later and refocus on my devotional and journaling)

Are you ready? If you've never kept a journal, I challenge you to throw your reservations to the wind and forge into the following pages. Besides, if writing about people, events, ideas, and thoughts was good enough for

Moses, David, and God, it's certainly good enough for you and me! Just plan to have an enriching time learning more about God, more about His current leading in your life, and more about yourself.

If you're already keeping a journal, why not start a second journal—one that will be a blessing to someone else as well as yourself (more about this in later chapters)?

In either case, get ready for some time out from the rat race, some mental R and R, some inexpensive emotional therapy, and maybe even a new ministry or two!

Get ready to write from your heart and to let God write on yours! Make some memories with Him today. Jot them down now so that later you can remember.

Part One

BASIC JOURNALING STYLES

"Your 'journal-istic' habits will develop as you go along."
—Leonard L. Knott★

EACH CHAPTER IN *WRITE IT ON YOUR HEART* will introduce one journaling method or style. A brief description of that method or style will precede each sample journal entry. Writing suggestions to get you started will follow each sample entry.

Remember, if you follow these suggestions, or use them as starting points for your own creative ideas, you will have a personal journal sampler by the time you finish this book.

In Part I we will look at three examples of common journaling styles:

1. The "Journalistic" Journal
2. The Emotional Response Journal
3. The Creative Writing Journal

You can incorporate any of these styles into your devotional times as well.

★ Leonard L. Knott, *Writing After Fifty* (Cincinnati, Ohio: Writer's Digest Books, 1985), p. 30.

Chapter 1

JUST THE FACTS, MA'AM!
(The Journalistic Journal)

*"The diary gets some of its strength by its innocent march
into the unknown future, step by step, day by day."*
—Theodore A. Rees Cheney ★

WHAT IS A "JOURNALISTIC" JOURNAL?

A Journalistic Journal is often no more than a loose collection of present and past memories recording the who, what, when, where, and why of everyday events. People often refer to this type of journal as a *diary*. Journal keepers may or may not relate their journal entries to a life lesson coming out of the experience.

The writing style is a straightforward laying out of the facts, succinctly stated. I first began keeping this type of journal in junior high when my mother gave me a diary-type journal for Christmas. I soon tired, however, of recording a litany of everyday events.

In college I again picked up my journal keeping and wrote intermittently. It helped me sort through—and remember—the more significant events of my busy young life. Occasionally I wrote about occurrences after the fact when they once again drifted through my memory.

The following entry (though a bit longer than most of the others) recalls a somewhat hair-raising experience from my first year in college.

THE JOURNALISTIC JOURNAL WRITING SAMPLE
"The 'Haunted' House"
(Or the Year I Learned to Hang in There)

During my freshman year in college I ended up, by default, in a newswriting class. The few students in this class served as the reporter pool for the school newspaper.

At the head of the table the stern wisp of a teacher (whom I'll call Dr. Detmore) informed us that one third of our quarter grade would depend on how many column inches we'd had published in the school paper. He informed us that 30 published inches a term would earn us only a C even if we did well on homework and exams.

Since my busy schedule and lack of assertiveness held me back from getting out and hustling stories, 30 published inches is *all* I eked out that first term. Used to A's and B's, this big fat C crushed me.

The next quarter I determined that sheer willpower could transform me into an aggressive reporter. I would rush my editor for early leads on campus stories. This effort resulted in 45 published inches. That brought my grade up to a much more acceptable B+.

However, right after we turned in our quarter's newspaper submission to Dr. Detmore, he gave us a reminder. The end-of-term story copies we handed him needed to be the exact ones we'd turned in to the newspaper office *before* the editor had worked on them. Oh, no! I hadn't remembered that stipulation!

An hour after class I stood before Dr. Detmore's desk. With a shaky voice I confessed that most of the copies I had given him had not been edited versions. He thanked me for sharing and announced that this admission had just backed my B+ down to a C for the second quarter in a row!

How I wanted to drop that stressful, frustrating class! Yet I couldn't.

During the first newswriting session of the spring quarter Dr. Detmore told us our main assignment (in addition to regular newspaper reporting) would be an undercover piece of "investigative reporting."

"What's that?" I naively asked.

"It's seeing something not easily explainable and *investigating* it," he responded, all but rolling his eyes. "Just get in there on your hands and knees and dig for the facts!"

I thought, *C No. 3 coming up!*

THE ABANDONED HOUSE

The next Sunday afternoon, to clear my brain between homework assignments, I took a brief hike up an isolated rural road. Suddenly, at a turn on this remote road I saw what someone would stereotypically refer to as a "haunted house."

"You need a subject for your investigative reporting article," I told myself, swallowing hard and trying to remain composed before this faded little clapboard structure with all the windows broken out.

I answered myself: "Like I'm going to investigate a haunted house?" Yet everything about this scenario silently screamed that a story was just waiting to be uncovered. I turned and fled. I didn't stop running until I was inside the front door of the dormitory.

I ran down to the room of my friend Nita (not her real

name). Bursting into her room, I asked, "Want to do some investigative reporting?"

Twenty minutes later we both slipped through the only outside door of the "haunted house," which led into a tiny kitchen. I looked at Nita, whose green eyes were wide. She followed me back into the kitchen and then followed my gaze up through a piece of ceiling hanging above the table.

I whispered, "Want to see what's up in the attic?"

Wordlessly she nodded, a glint of adventure coming into her eyes.

I whispered, "If the kitchen table is sturdy enough to hold us, maybe we can pull ourselves up." We helped each other up and saw, in the pale light shining through a high attic window, an old trunk.

Carefully we lifted the trunk lid and then removed the top tray, which was water stained and covered with patches of green mold.

Across the bottom of the trunk lay scattered old postcards and pages of long-ago correspondence. Vandals had stripped all the stamps from the postcards and envelopes. Closer examination revealed why. Most had been posted from an exotic little Asian kingdom. A number were written to or by a Miss Clara Jade.

"Let's take some with us," I suggested. Nita and I each stuffed a few cards and sheets of paper into the pockets of our jackets.

Just then the back door slammed shut. "Let's get out of here!" I said.

Nita nodded and balanced her way to the hole above the kitchen table.

Later that week a school librarian helped me locate the name of Miss Clara Jade in old church yearbooks. Having been briefly acquainted with Miss Jade while in that area on furlough during mission service, the librarian was able to tell me the woman had eventually married. Before long she recalled Miss Jade's married name and then helped me trace the woman's current whereabouts—someplace back East.

When Dr. Detmore called on me the following Tuesday for a progress report on my investigative article, I began telling him what I had discovered.

"You did what?" he roared. "Breaking and entering on someone else's property?"

But I *could* tell he *was* interested.

Dr. Detmore helped me get permission from the proper authorities to gather long-lost correspondence from the house (known originally as the Byrd House, named after the original builders).

I was able to contact Miss Jade by mail and later by telephone. She was thrilled to be reunited with long-lost family correspondence from a trunk that had "disappeared" many years earlier.

She also gave me the lowdown on my "haunted" house. In the process she brought to light a number of long-forgotten names and church-related events associated with the old house before it had fallen on harder times.

More than any other early life experience, that one taught me that perseverance pays! My investigative article about the historic Byrd House piqued great interest among the students as well as in the community.

Best of all, however, I finally earned that elusive A in newswriting class.

JOURNALISTIC JOURNAL—YOUR TURN

Pick up your favorite pen or boot up your computer and try one of these:

- ✏ Write three sentences about something you did today (be sure to include colors, aromas, and sounds).
- ✏ Recall a time when life taught you an interesting lesson.
- ✏ Relive an event that helped you better understand yourself.

---

* Theodore A. Rees Cheney, *Writing Creative Nonfiction* (Cincinnati: Writer's Digest Books, 1987), p. 146.

Chapter 2

OUCH! THAT HURT!

(The Emotional Response Journal)

*"The strongest, most lasting memories
are those embedded in emotion."*
—Theodore A. Rees Cheney ★

WHAT IS AN EMOTIONAL RESPONSE JOURNAL?

An Emotional Response Journal is a safe place to record one's emotional responses (both positive and negative) to what one observes and experiences, sort of a journalistic journal with a heart.

The writing style is very personal and highly subjective in tone. I have found that this type of journal—more than any of the others—helps me to make sense out of difficult events and situations in my life.

THE EMOTIONAL RESPONSE JOURNAL
WRITING SAMPLE
"Watch Out for Anesthesia!"

I didn't even feel my injury until an hour after I left the dentist's office today. As far as dental visits go, I've got it made. Restful music, a professionally muted color scheme, friendly technicians, and of course, the well-read, urbane dentist. I ended my visit as I always do: comfortably medicated, my personhood intact, and with the refreshing cinnamon-flavored taste of the final rinse still tingling under my tongue.

It was *after* I'd been away from the dental office for a couple of hours, however, that the problem started. No, it wasn't just the anesthesia wearing off that caused me pain. It was that place on the inside of my previously deadened left cheek where I'd unconsciously been gnawing.

Oh, dear! I thought. *I was going to treat myself to a spicy Mexican lunch for a postdental reward. But now those jalapeño peppers would burn me at the stake! How dumb! Why wasn't I more careful about what I was doing?*

Suddenly I realized I often make the same mistake in my spiritual life. The subtle, pleasurable tingling of sin quiets my sensitive spiritual nerves. Anesthetized by the latest cultural perspective blowing across the airwaves, I unconsciously nibble away at a deadened conscience until a moment of clarity (often a bit painful) shocks me back to reality.

Right after the September 11 terrorist attacks, I remember hearing a snatch of radio interview. A New York reporter on the street was stopping passersby for their reactions. One of the interviewees just happened to be an actress with one foot already inside Broadway's promising door.

Tears in her voice, the young woman bemoaned, "I suddenly see I've been wasting my life on the superficial—it's all been about me. I'm feeling so shallow and ashamed! This tragedy has woken me up. From now on I'm going to make my life count for something that really matters."

My dental visit today reminded me that I want to do the same.

THE EMOTIONAL RESPONSE JOURNAL—YOUR TURN

Pick up your favorite pen and see what you come up with for the following:

~ Describe something you have recently observed or experienced. How did it make you feel? Has this emotional experience enabled you to view life from an unusual perspective you might not have previously considered? Practically applied, what will this new perspective "look like" in your everyday life?

---

* Theodore A. Rees Cheney, *Writing Creative Nonfiction*, p. 3.

Chapter 3

IT WAS A DARK
AND STORMY NIGHT . . .

(The Creative Writing Journal)

*"Dramatic writing has a key ingredient
that distinguishes life from nonlife,
the snake from the stick—motion, action."*
—Theodore A. Rees Cheney ★

WHAT IS A CREATIVE WRITING JOURNAL?

A Creative Writing Journal provides a haven for individuality and freestyle writing. When I have time, I like to observe human nature and record it, embellished with description, punctuated by dialogue, and approached from unusual perspectives.

When I asked my high school students to keep journals (free of the restrictive conventions of punctuation and capitalization, if they so chose) some confided that this type of writing was the most useful to them. They felt that normal writing restrictions also restricted creative thinking.

By the way, a middle-aged woman from a church I once attended confided that she had a special journal in which she kept her "creative erotic writing," whatever *that* meant (I didn't go there).

I'd like to suggest that a Christian's writing will prove much more of a personal blessing, much more significant, and much more spiritually enduring when the writer follows two guidelines. First, preface any writing activity by prayer. Then keep journal contents in accordance with biblical principles (Phil. 4:8).

The writing style in a Creative Writing Journal is whatever the creative journal keeper wants it to be: narrative, short story, drama, poetry, dialogue, stream-of-consciousness, or a mixture. For life and color, be sure to include details that contribute to "motion" and "action," in the words of the author previously quoted.

THE CREATIVE WRITING JOURNAL SAMPLES

The following is the beginning of a true story, written for young children, about my father and the only cat he ever owned.

SAMPLE 1: "BOPPA AND THE CAT"

"That does it!" exclaimed the tall man with the silver hair. "Grandma, I'm going to get a cat!"

"Why, Boppa," said a short woman with a clear voice. "All these years you have said that cats belong on the farm. Why would you get a cat now?"

"Come with me, and I will show you." Boppa led Grandma through the garage. She smiled as he shuffled out the front garage door in his old bedroom slippers and worn surgical pants. This was his gardening outfit. Boppa never cared what the neighbors thought.

Boppa stopped abruptly and pointed toward a mound of fresh brown dirt setting atop his smooth green lawn. "That is why I am going to get a cat! Gophers are ruining my lawn!"

Grandma followed his hand as he pointed out yet another hole and then another.

"But Boppa," asked Grandma, "how will you and a cat get along? For years you've said that you don't have time for cats."

Boppa made quick decisions. Cats have to think a long time before making a move.

Boppa liked to give orders. Cats don't take orders—from *anyone*.

"Tomorrow," announced Boppa, "we're going to the animal pound to get a cat to help me with my yardwork!"

Oh, thought Grandma, *how will Boppa and a cat ever get along?*

⮑ ⮑ ⮑

The following are examples of how I might have written the Byrd House account from chapter 1 in a creative writing style, sharing more specifics and emotion-laden descriptions.

SAMPLE 2: "THE HAUNTED HOUSE—AMPLIFIED"

On the walk before I saw the house: A windy March drizzle tugged at—and splattered over—my pink umbrella. I watched my galoshes kick through rain puddles and wondered what on earth I could investigate for newswriting class.

Hearing a distant rumble of thunder, I thought, *This is kind of a spooky day.*

Just then a sharp turn in the narrow road made me look up from my feet. What I saw directly before me nearly buckled my knees in fear.

There, perched on a reinforced rock bank, was the smallest, narrowest, darkest, scariest-looking "haunted house" I'd ever seen!

Dark-gray mold spread across the white clapboard beneath the eaves.

Shredded wisps of curtains flapped and fluttered through the gaping windows edged by shards of glass. I saw no roadfront entrance to the house.

Exhaling, I looked about me. I was very much alone. I heard no vehicle coming from either direction—only the whining of the wind through the attic windows.

I took a deep breath and jumped across the roadside ditch onto a landing at the bottom of a cracked concrete staircase.

I hope nobody's watching me from inside, I thought, my throat suddenly dry.

Careful not to slip on the green slimy moss, I climbed the narrow stairs and tiptoed around to the other side of the house until I reached the back—and only—door.

Quietly I closed my umbrella and knocked. All I heard in response through the broken window was the slight echo of my timid tap.

I cleared my throat. "Anybody home?"

The only sound in response was rain dripping from the eaves over my head.

I cautiously twisted the doorknob. The door swung slowly open.

Then something inside the house creaked. I mean— *really* creaked!

❧ ❧ ❧

After I knocked at my girlfriend's dormitory room: "Come in!" she yelled.

When I entered, she looked up from her desk and said, "Your hair's all wet." (Only then did I realize I'd forgotten to open my umbrella on my quick escape from the little house on the hill.)

"Besides that," she continued, "you look like you've just seen a ghost!"

"Nita," I said, still panting, "I don't know about any ghost, but I've just knocked on the door of a *very* scary-looking house."

What?" she exclaimed?

❧ ❧ ❧

When Nita and I are back to explore the house: The stench of mold made us put our jacket collars to our noses. Kitchen appliances had long since been ripped from the walls, though a shaky chair and dilapidated table remained.

Silently we tiptoed across remnants of a damp living-room rug, past a filthy little bathroom, and into the only bedroom. The bedstead rose above broken beer bottles and ankle-deep trash. Rusty wire coils and soiled cotton batting poked up through the stained, molding mattress.

Up in the attic: A brisk wind whipped about our faces as it blew through the front attic window and out the back one. Wet sheets of paper and old postcards lay scattered about the "floor."

Careful to walk only on the beams (so we wouldn't fall through the rotted ceiling), we made our way toward two pieces of plywood laid across two of the beams. On the far side of the plywood stood a black leather trunk.

Nita and I looked at each other. In a low whisper she asked, "Forgotten treasure or something we don't want to see?"

THE CREATIVE WRITING JOURNAL—YOUR TURN

Pick up your favorite pen or boot up your computer and try one of these:

- A snatch of dialogue between two friends who haven't seen each other for 15 years
- One of Christ's shorter parables placed in a modern setting
- Whatever comes to your mind concerning a favorite topic of yours
- Your first day in heaven.
- A story about an incident you once observed

---

* Theodore A. Rees Cheney, *Writing Creative Nonfiction,* p. 13.

Part Two

POTENTIAL GIFT/ MINISTRY JOURNALS

MY "BOPPA AND THE CAT" entry eventually turned into a self-illustrated book for my father the following Christmas. Not only did he appreciate the time I'd put into it, the entire family enjoyed reliving how a little gray cat named Penelope had mellowed his once-staunch position against felines.

Proverbs 11:25 states that whoever "refreshes others will himself be refreshed" (NIV). In Part II of *Write It on Your Heart* we will examine four of my favorite journal types that also have potential for refreshing others. I love these because not only do they contain limitless friendship and comfort-ministry potential, they also refresh the soul of the journal keeper.

- The Poetry Journal
- The Purposeful Recall Journal
- The Family Heirloom Journal
- The Blessings Journal

We hope and pray that you'll enjoy keeping at least one of these types of journals as much as we have!

Chapter 4

ROSES ARE RED/ VIOLETS ARE BLUE

(The Poetry Journal)

"Poetry is the spontaneous overflow of powerful feelings."
—William Wordsworth[1]

"Of all those arts in which the wise excel,
Nature's chief masterpiece is writing well."
—John Sheffield[2]

WHAT IS A POETRY JOURNAL?

A Poetry Journal can be similar to any of the other types of journals we've already discussed, but with one main difference. Instead of writing prose, the journal keeper treats the topics of choice poetically.

While learning to live with loneliness and transition during a very solitary time in my life, I began writing clandestine poetry. It grew into a private volume of 200-plus poems, which I entitled *Thoughts From the Levee*. I gave it that title because I'd slip to a nearby bird preserve during occasional free hours on weekends, sit on a levee, and write my thoughts in a journal.

Thoughts From the Levee became for me—at that point in my life—free emotional and spiritual therapy, an

uplifting Sabbath afternoon activity, an unobtrusive travel-
ing companion in my backpack or car, a new hobby, and
a self-taught class.

So what does a poetry journal have to do with gifts,
comfort, or ministry?

Has anyone ever handed you a poem and said, "I
wrote this for you"? When I did this for a student once,
she began to cry. "Nobody ever wrote a poem about me
before," she said. "I feel so special."

To be perfectly honest, I must admit that at the present
season of my life, I rarely write a poem. It just doesn't
meet my needs. Yet it certainly did about four years running at one point.

Here is the beauty of a Poetry Journal.

The writing style is *whatever* you want it to be! How's
that for freedom? Remember, a poem does *not* have to
rhyme. It does *not* have to be confined to strict meter.
Some of the world's most beautifully flowing, and even
staccato-paced, poems are the ones King David wrote. In
the minds of many "The Song of Solomon," penned by
David's son Solomon, is the most sumptuous love poem of
all time—and it never rhymed, even in its original language.

If you want to be more technical with your poetry
writing, you can find "how-to" writing books at most
bookstores. You can pick up one of these paperbacks for a
few dollars. If you absolutely *must* rhyme your poems, you
might want to take advantage of an inexpensive paperback
rhyming dictionary.

Here's something else exciting about writing poems in
a journal. You *never* know where one of your journal en-

tries may lead. Though emotional and spiritual therapy— *not* publication—was the original purpose of my poetry writing, around 20 of them have appeared in various books, collections, and devotionals. My late friend Phydella Hogan published her first book of original poetry, *Matchsticks,* at the age of 73. In writer's guides for both the religious and secular markets you can find information about publications that publish original poetry.[3]

Again, a poem is anything you want it to be!

POETRY JOURNAL WRITING SAMPLES ("I FELL IN LOVE WITH THE FOREST," AND OTHER POEMS)

The following sad observance refers to the possible reason for an acquaintance's failed relationship:

"Success in Love"
success in love?
the chance was slim—
since they were both
in love . . . with him

Our culture's love affair with romantic sentimentalism overlooks a thousand other sources of emotional fulfillment:

"Once I Thought"
once I thought
a snowy forest,
fresh and pure,
would be the perfect place
to fall in love—
so I fell in love . . .
with the forest

Write It on Your Heart

Considering the big picture when it comes to love is crucial to a lasting relationship:

"The Real Thing"
It's light—the energy
It takes
To love someone
For a day—
But have you weighed
The effort
It takes
For a lifetime?

A springtime northern California gibbis (the opposite of a *crescent* in the monthly moon cycle) inspired "Reflection on a Waning Gibbis" (a haiku):[4]

silent, silver shafts—
long-shadowed moongirl, weeping,
bathes the broken night

Poetry is a powerful tool for ongoing introspection:

"Every Day"
every day
i find out
more and more
about the person
i didn't know
i am

As I once contemplated a museum lava flow demonstration with my students, this thought came to mind about God's working:

"Lava Flow"
Melting,
Bonding,
Sealing,
Coating smooth—
The persistent lava flow
Has its way with the hard, cold ground
Beneath its advancing glow—
As does His Word
Upon this rock-rough
Heart

A well-known chess master (and author) has nothing on the Creator when it comes to spectacular "moves." I used rhyme in "developing the pieces":

developing the pieces
and when to move the rook—
questions that are answered
in Pandolfini's book

on others he keeps silent—
the Master must surprise
hope cocooned within the soul,
discovered butterflies

You might try imitating the style of a poet you appreciate. One of my favorite poets was a Renaissance metaphysical poet. The brilliant George Herbert turned down international recognition and riches as a British court poet. He chose, rather, to serve God as a country pastor all his life. The following poem is my humble attempt to imitate one of his poetic styles:

> "Daylight Saving Time"
> Foolish time expenditure!
> I know not where it went—
> That gratifying interval
> With Thee today I spent.
> Lost? (three hours—alone with Thee)
> Or saved up for eternity?

And finally, Romans 8:28 suggested this thimble-sized poem:

> "Burden"
> the snail's
> burden
> is also
> his refuge

THE POETRY JOURNAL—YOUR TURN

Why write poetry?

My answer to that question is Why not? I've discovered that if one is out of control over many things in life, she can *still* be in charge of her pen! She can have . . .

> "Ultimate Control"
> Absolute,
> Despotic—
> This pen
> Performs
> My (capricious)
> Will

So go ahead! At least try a four-word poem (three adjectives and an object), such as this one:

Pink

Purple

Yellow . . .

Bouquet

Now write a similar poem about a person for whom you care. Then, turn this poem into a mini-encouragement ministry by sending it to the person about whom it was written.

Refresh a heart—and be refreshed in return!

---

[1] William Wordsworth, *Lyrical Ballads,* preface, quoted in *The Pocket Book of Quotations,* ed. Henry Davidoff, (New York: Pocket Books, 1969), p. 285.

[2] John Sheffield, *Essay on Poetry,* quoted in *Christianity Today,* April 22, 2002, p. 79.

[3] Sally E. Stuart, *Christian Writers' Market Guide 2003* (updated annually) (Colorado Springs, Colo.: Shaw Books, 2003). Look under "Poetry" in the index.

[4] Popular form of Japanese poetry.

Chapter 5

ONCE UPON A MEMORY
(The Purposeful Recall Journal)

*"Fond Memory brings the light
Of other days around me."*
—Thomas Moore *

WHAT IS A PURPOSEFUL RECALL JOURNAL?

The Purposeful Recall Journal is a collection of happy and poignant memories concerning a specific person in your life.

A Purposeful Recall Journal can also become a tool for personal encouragement for someone going through tough times. One of my journals, in which I kept humorous real-life anecdotes (some from my own adventures), resulted in *Diary for a Doctor*. I sent this journal to my first back surgeon, a kind, godly man who loved to laugh. Since he was battling the final months of a fast-growing cancer, my journal ended with a lengthy tribute to the difference his efforts had made not only in my life but in the lives of my students.

Some time later the doctor's wife told me he kept the little journal by his bedside, reading and rereading it during his final weeks. He said it always lifted his spirits.

The Early Years, originally a diary about first-grade follies, became a gift for my first-grade teacher, when she became bedridden 30 years later and crippled with arthritis.

Several of my memory journals have evolved into hand-written books as gifts for others. *Grandma Lucile,* a self-published book, is a story that evolved from journal entries I wrote about my mother when she was a little girl. She loved seeing her childhood story clumsily illustrated (I'm not an artist) and "bound" between stationery-store leatherette covers.

The writing style of the Purposeful Recall Journal is anecdotal. A series of short anecdotes and memories form the tapestry for this warm quilt of memories.

THE PURPOSEFUL RECALL JOURNAL WRITING SAMPLE
"Mrs. Tupper"

One of the greatest disappointments in my life was the day my parents told me I couldn't take my first-grade teacher with me to the second grade. How I wept!

Mrs. Tupper had become for me the epitome of every safe and wonderful thing to be found outside of one's own home. Though I didn't know all these words then, the name "Teacher," as exemplified by Mrs. Tupper, also meant friend, protector, example, comforter, cheerleader, guide, counselor, laughter, security, forgiveness, silent sufferer, and beauty.

I adored my first-grade teacher as I had never adored anyone before. She taught me phonics, John 14:1-3, and how to bow gracefully after a piano solo.

When callous classmates wounded my fragile feelings, Mrs. Tupper said, "Those were only words."

When I screamed over a painfully scraped knee, she got down at face level, dressed the wound, and whispered, "It will heal."

When assertive classmate Gina (not her real name) strong-armed me to the ground in the girls' cloakroom so she could perform a "tonsillectomy" on me with a clothes hanger, Mrs. Tupper visited my home the next day. In my parents' presence she declared, "You don't *ever* have to do anything wrong or stupid that someone else wants you to do."

Mrs. Tupper is the reason—15 years after I first met her—other girls and boys began calling me "Teacher" too.

THE PURPOSEFUL RECALL JOURNAL—YOUR TURN

Why just write something and let it lie fallow, to be lost in the shadows of time? A Purposeful Recall Journal about someone holds such wonderful possibilities for encouraging and affirming him or her! This type of journal takes no more time to keep than any other.

In fact, I have several journals going at once (as you might be doing now in this journal sampler). I write in one journal one day and in another on another day, as the mood or need strikes me.

Pick up your favorite pen. Try the following and prepare to be blessed—by blessing someone else.

- List three to five people (yet living) about whom you have positive, significant memories.
- Under each name, note abbreviated anecdotes regarding some positive experiences with them.
- Decide which one could use the most encouragement right now.
- Determine when would be an appropriate time to remind this person what a wonderful difference

he/she has made in your life (birthday, Christmas, or just any time).

↝ Start a purposeful recall journal for that person.

★ Thomas Moore, *The Light of Other Days,* quoted in *The Pocket Book of Quotations,* ed. Henry Davidoff, p. 224.

Chapter 6

COOKING WITH WORDS

(The Family Heirloom Journal)

"The keeper of the diary, journal, or some other form of log may use it some day simply as one source of information to help him or her write an autobiography or memoir."
—Theodore A. Rees Cheney[1]

WHAT IS A FAMILY HEIRLOOM JOURNAL?[2]

The Family Heirloom Journal is a collection of happy and poignant memories concerning one's interaction with *family members.*

One of Penny Wheeler's engaging editorials in *Women of Spirit* magazine described how she annotated her cookbooks. In the margins beside favorite family recipes she noted dates and events for which she had prepared those dishes. What a wonderful legacy to pass on to her children!

Years after the death of my mother, Mabelle Sherrig, I (Lucile Roth) began keeping a memory journal about her. My journal met several needs at that point in my life. First, it gave me an early retirement project to fill the empty places in my days. Second, the project helped me bring closure to the loss of my mother. Finally, my journal developed into three years of wonderful Christmas gifts for my family.

How? My Family Heirloom Journal, with its 60-plus entries, grew into a collection of vignettes about my own early life as well as about my close relationship with Mother. This journal preserved family history that would have been lost had I not taken the time to write it down.

One can also ghostwrite a Family Heirloom Journal. My daughter Carolyn wrote a journal from the perspective of her son when he was 13. *Memoirs of a Missionary Kid* became our Christmas present from him that year. How we loved it!

Since I am legally blind now, my copy of "his" journal has reverted back to him. He is excited to have had so many of his early-childhood African adventures recorded and plans to share them with his children when they come along.

Another variation of the Family Heirloom Journal is an annotated family photo album. Before losing my sight, I put together 16 annotated journal photo albums for family members. These include ancestral and historical anecdotes, dates, and other information.

Believe me, a Family Heirloom Journal is a gift that keeps on giving!

The writing style of the Family Heirloom Journal is anecdotal—family stories and memories you want to preserve for future generations.

THE FAMILY HEIRLOOM JOURNAL WRITING SAMPLE

I once wrote, "One of my biggest joys in life ever since I left home in 1938 has been corresponding with my mom."

Of course, I no longer had this outlet after my mother was killed in a tragic automobile accident. Yet I still enjoyed recording, on colorful journal pages, events my mother would have liked hearing about had she yet been alive. The following are a few excerpts from my family heirloom journals.

"Dearest Mom"

January 7, 1997: "Hurray! I just did it! Fifty-two years after you paid for swimming lessons for me at the Jewish Community Center in Omaha, I called the YWCA and surreptitiously scheduled my first swimming lesson. My overwhelming horror of water through the years might have stemmed from the lifesaving drill for the crew of the San Francisco ferry in 1932. I thought we were all being evacuated and was sure I wouldn't be able to find my folks on the deck during all the excitement.

"I can still feel the Golden Gate gusts that blew through my white wool coat and embroidered blue sailor hat you bought me for the trip to General Conference. After the drill you found us children and good-naturedly pointed out that the crew was already putting lifeboats back on the racks. You chuckled over our childishness, but my 12-year-old insides were filled with frozen fear. Today—a half century later—I buried that freezing fear in the warm YWCA pool."

February 25, 1997: "I wanted to surprise two of my grandchildren who graduated from college in June of 1994. So I found out who their heroes and cultural role models were. I had celebrities (boy, it was hard getting addresses!) send their congratulatory wishes directly to the respective college addresses.

"The kids heard from Milton Friedman, a recent Nobel Memorial Prize winner in economics, Olympic gold medalist speed skater Dan Jansen, the president of the

Write It on Your Heart

United States, Mickey and Minnie Mouse, the queen of England, Tom Landry of the Dallas Cowboys, and Elizabeth Dole, as well as a number of other cultural luminaries. The actress Angela Lansbury sent my granddaughter a belated handwritten congratulatory card because the elderly actress had been in the hospital having surgery when my request arrived. My grandchildren have put these cards and letters into special scrapbooks and tell me they get such pleasure leafing through them after all these years."

THE FAMILY HEIRLOOM JOURNAL—YOUR TURN

Pick up your favorite pen.

Make a list of poignant, significant, fun, and memorable events you would like your descendants to remember (or know) about your ancestors or your own life experiences. As you find time, begin writing about one of these.

---

[1] Theodore A. Rees Cheney, *Writing Creative Nonfiction,* pp. 146, 147.
[2] Chapter by Lucile Roth.

Chapter 7

ASHES TO BEAUTY AND MOURNING TO JOY

(The Blessings Journal)

"But thou art holy, O thou that inhabitest the praises of Israel."
—Ps. 22:3

"To give unto them beauty for ashes, the oil of joy for mourning."
—Isa. 61:3

WHAT IS A BLESSINGS JOURNAL?

The Blessings Journal is a collection, list, or record of God's blessings as you recall, or become aware of, them.

How easy it is for us to concentrate on the "ashes" in our lives when God wants us to see the beauty. How often we forget to pour the "oil of joy" over our mourning.

I once heard a doctor give this prescription: "Whenever you are tempted to become depressed or wallow in self-pity, grab a pen and make a list of 10 things for which you are grateful. I guarantee that you will start feeling better right away!"

I have followed his advice—many times. I've noticed that I have a hard time stopping at 10 items when I make my lists. Sometimes I list blessings for 10 minutes instead!

The writing style of the Blessings Journal is any format

that works for you. I have a number of 10-item segments. Sometimes I elaborate on one of the listed items. As I thumb through the pages of my Blessings Journal I notice I have also interspersed my lists with short anecdotes about events or people that have been blessings to me.

I keep my Blessings Journal as a secondary journal. Usually I add to it on dreary days or during those times when I'm tempted to wallow in self-pity. My mother has done the same.

THE BLESSINGS JOURNAL WRITING SAMPLES

The following comes from a "Blessings" section in one of my (Carolyn's) journals.

SAMPLE 1: "BLESSINGS"

A 10-item blessings list: husband, sons, mother, daughter–in–law, aunt, in–laws, eyesight, birdsongs, trees, fresh air.

A 10-minute blessings list: cell phones, church family, hiking, the gift of personal choice, the Holy Spirit, Bible, obstacles, creativity, kittens, hope, God's covenant of grace, wild turkeys, treadmill, dobro, cooking, God's faithfulness, gardening magazines, sewing machine, church organ, human love, divine love, an upstairs balcony, modern medicine, strength to get through tough times, girlfriends to cheer me up, redemption, squirrels, waterfalls, a safe and happy childhood, a sense of my spiritual heritage, a sense of my geneological heritage, the Lord's Prayer, the resurrection morning when the righteous will see God's face and be satisfied (Ps. 17:15), summertime corn on the cob, olive oil, home-cured green olives, butterflies, camp meetings, grape-sized tomatoes, grapefruit-sized tomatoes, church potlucks, angelhair pasta with pesto sauce, fresh garden herbs, deer in the wild, pansies and wisteria, stamping, homemade greeting cards, good neighbors, shopping, organic food markets, a walking partner, billowy clouds, spring rain . . . . well, you get the idea.

SAMPLE 2: "INTO THE LIGHT"

My mother, Lucile, dictated most of this journal entry to my father after she became legally blind. She dictated the final paragraphs to me during the fourth year of her blindness.

Crawling out of bed, I glanced—as I always did—at the double frame holding photographs of my mother and father. That morning, however, the frames appeared to be empty. I rubbed my eyes, bent over, and looked again more closely.

Again . . . Nothing.

My pulse starting to race; I straightened up and looked at my face in the mirror. I saw nothing there, either! It was as if I had completely disappeared!

I called out to my husband. "I can't see a thing directly in front of my eyes!"

He couldn't begin to grasp what I was telling him— even several hours later when, at a restaurant, he handed me a menu I could no longer read. Within the week an eye specialist confirmed the permanence of my vision loss. On the way home from the doctor's office, in the midst of Los Angeles rush-hour freeway traffic, my husband burst into tears and wept inconsolably.

Latent macular degeneration had finally manifested

itself in my permanent, literal, and overnight loss of vision. During the following weeks I sometimes experienced strong peripheral (but double) vision interrupted by blinding colored lights behind my closed eyelids. The worst was seeing horrifying distortions when I gazed sorrowfully at beloved faces once so familiar to me.

I could not bear putting my parents' photographs away, though I tried not to look at them anymore. Somehow I had to face the harsh reality that the only way I would ever see them clearly on this earth would be through memory's eye.

When I was born in 1917, my parents had named me Lucile, which means "shining light." Now, from within my encroaching darkness, my very name taunted me as being yet another cruel twist of fate.

THE HARDEST CHOICE OF MY LIFE

Always an avid reader, my life as an English teacher had overflowed with ever-expanding knowledge, activity, and a sense of purpose. I loved being surrounded by youthful minds thriving on the give-and-take of the classroom. However, a few years earlier, a cataract surgery gone awry had forced me to resign at the beginning of what was to have been my forty-fourth—and final—year in the classroom.

To help fill the void left by my involuntarily early retirement, I learned how to make greeting and condolence cards. Sending them to people with hurting hearts helped fill the void left by my untimely departure from teaching. Sometimes I'd even pretty up a sale teddy bear with a bow and send it along with the card. Now, however, I couldn't even see well enough to tie a simple bow!

In the wake of my sudden blindness, I experienced a sense of indescribable shock. At times the humiliating changes this life-altering handicap demanded plunged me beneath waves of despair. Staying in bed all day seemed far preferable to rising when it meant having to grope my way through yet another dark and purposeless day.

Though I had not chosen to stand at this particular cross-roads in my life, only I could choose the direction my mind and heart would take from this point on. And that decision would make all the difference in the world—both for me and for those around me.

My unavoidable choice was to embrace either hope or despair.

No decision in my life ever required more faith and courage than this one did. After months of desperate struggle, I chose hope—because hope brings blessings.

THE NITTY-GRITTY

The only way I knew how to "choose" hope was to practice it. I did so in the following three ways.

Despite my newly imposed blindness, I *reflected on God's promises.* More than "reflect," I had to literally cling to His stated commitment in 1 Corinthians 10:13, that He wouldn't permit me to suffer beyond that which I could bear.

Two years later, following the death of my husband (of 63 years), I was reassured that my Maker promised to be not only my guide for the remainder of my life (Ps. 48:14) but also my husband (Isa. 54:5).

Another way I chose hope was by reflecting on

Christ's actions—especially when my age-related rheumatoid arthritis and bursitis added to a sense of increased darkness. If Christ, while enduring unspeakable suffering on the cross, would make provision for the care of His elderly mother, certainly—by one means or another—He would take care of me.

Finally, I chose hope by learning how to *reach out to others* the best I could.

BEARLY THERE

All around me were people experiencing significant events in their lives, either traumatic or celebratory. Though I could no longer see well enough to tie bows around the necks of teddy bears, I could *feel* to dress them.

I suppose someone else could drop them in the mail for me, I mused. With that, God dropped a whole new "ministry" into my lap—my own burden bear outreach. I can hardly believe the difference it's made in my life.

When I start feeling sorry for myself, I've learned to do something immediately for someone else. Just as quickly, despair ceases to be an option. Carolyn's little poem with accompanying Bible promises suspended from the necks of bears destined for people in grief or trauma also feeds my soul:

I've come to keep you company—
To shed a tear or two.
To let you hold my tiny paw
For what you're going through.
But most of all, here's why I've come—
It's this I want to share.
Keep Jesus in your heart and thoughts.

He will your burdens bear.
(See 1 Peter. 5:7 and Romans 8:28.)

"Listen to this, Mom!" Carolyn recently exclaimed. "Just for fun I made a list of all the bears you've given away over the past three and a half years. On an average, you've sent off one bear every 7.3 days! You're almost up to 200!"

That's 200 times God has given *me* an extraspecial blessing. I'm amazed that my bears now reside in such far-flung places as Romania, El Salvador, and the Philippines.

SURPRISE!

Yes, my visual world continues to darken. On this earth, I will never again look into the eyes of my children and grandchildren. And even in a well-lighted mirror, I am still as "invisible" as I was on the day I first went blind. Yet God continues to remind me of His loving care through daily blessings—and one big surprise.

One day, several months after that first horrifying morning of blindness, I involuntarily glanced in the direction of my parents' portraits. To my amazement, I saw them clearly—in their gold frames—without any distortion whatsoever.

Mother's soft curls about her gentle face . . .

Dad's clear blue eyes . . .

I feared I was hallucinating, so I said nothing to anyone that day, or the next.

Yet several years later I can *still* see God's love for me in the eyes of my parents when I look at their portraits each morning! This continuing gift from God reminds me, on a daily basis, to choose—to *practice*—hope.

Write It on Your Heart

It also reminds me to be true to the name my parents gave me so long ago. The name, Lucile ("shining light"), no longer taunts my visual challenges. Rather it reminds me that no matter how dark life may get, God will still help me to let my light shine.

THE BLESSINGS JOURNAL—YOUR TURN

Follow the "blessing" doctor's advice. Do one of the following:

- ☙ Make a list of 10 things (including people, situations, events, or items) for which you are grateful. Do this for at least three days in a row.
- ☙ Twice this week, write continuously for 10 minutes about some of your greatest blessings.
- ☙ Recall and then record a time when God brought blessing out of brokenness.

Part Three

DEVOTIONAL
ENHANCEMENT JOURNALS

ALTHOUGH MOTHER AND I ENJOY ALL the previous journaling methods, the ones in this section are my favorite because each at different times has helped enrich my spiritual
life.

In Part III of *Write It on Your Heart,* we will examine six devotional enhancement journaling styles. We
hope that your keeping one or more of them will both
deepen and sweeten your relationship with Jesus.

- The Conversations-With-God Journal
- The Collection Journal
- The Prayer Request Journal
- The Spiritual Weapons Arsenal Journal
- The Needful Subjects Journal
- The Scripture Memorization Journal

Chapter 8

DEAR BEST FRIEND . . .

(The Conversations-With-God Journal)

"Come now, and let us reason together."
—God[1]

"Draw nigh to God, and he will draw nigh to you."
—The apostle James[2]

WHAT IS A CONVERSATIONS-WITH-GOD JOURNAL?

The Conversations-With-God Journal is simply talking to God—through writing—as you would to an intimate friend. Some people refer to this method as "writing out your prayers."

Any conversation involves at least two parties. God speaks most clearly to us through His Word. Since we desire to discerningly "hear" His Word, we always want to first pray for the presence of His Spirit to be with us before we open the Bible.

Pastor Dwight Nelson suggests that after we do this, we begin reading. When a text or passage of Scripture "speaks" to us, we copy it down using one color of ink. Then, using another color ink, we write our next part of the "conversation."

The writing style of the Conversations-With-God Journal is personal, reflective, and introspective.

THE CONVERSATIONS-WITH-GOD WRITING SAMPLE
"The Conversation"

God to me (in blue ink): "For I am the Lord your God. You shall therefore consecrate yourselves, and you shall be holy; for I am holy. . . . You shall therefore be holy, for I *am* holy" (Lev. 11:44, 45, NKJV).

Me to God (in red pencil): Dear Father, You love me so much! Even when I'm a hopeless captive to sin. Yet You continue the slow, laborious task of redeeming me!

On top of that, You honor me by saying that You want my character to resemble Yours! You want *me* to look like *You!*

My feeble defenses against You are disarmed by such unspeakable love. I surrender. Take me. Make me holy. Help me to know You better.

THE CONVERSATIONS-WITH-GOD JOURNAL—YOUR TURN

Pick up your favorite pen and try one of these:

- Begin reading a familiar Bible passage. When a thought or verse jumps out at you, stop. Copy it down. Then reflect on it and respond to it as you would respond to a friend in a conversation.
- Begin reading an unfamiliar Bible chapter. In writing, talk to God about anything you're reading that applies to your life today.

---

[1] Isa. 1:18.

[2] James 4:8.

Chapter 9

AN ENCOURAGING WORD

(The Collection Journal)

"So the carpenter encouraged the goldsmith."
—Isa. 41:7

WHAT IS A COLLECTION JOURNAL?

A Collection Journal is one in which you can jot down encouraging, motivating, and helpful quotes. This is a comforting journal to refer to on dark days.

The writing style of a Collection Journal isn't any one style, as the journal is simply a compilation of quotes that have meaning to you.

Ministry possibility flash! I once read of a woman who finds and annotates one quote a day. She notes the date (without the year) and jots down the same quote on three or four different index cards. At the end of the year she gives away her extra sets as Christmas gifts to friends or family members who are going through tough times.

COLLECTION JOURNAL WRITING SAMPLE

"To pray is to change."[1]

"The revival must come from above. . . . If we return to the Lord with our whole heart, He will revive us."[2]

"Joy is not a feeling; it is a choice. It is not based upon circumstances; it is based upon attitude. It is free, but it is not cheap. It is the by-product of a growing relationship with Jesus Christ. . . . It requires commitment, courage, and endurance."[3]

"When I am fearful or anxious for myself, I pray for others. I pray for everyone who comes into my thoughts. . . . My fear soon disappears. Interceding for others releases me."[4]

"Second, remember that we must keep our priorities in focus. We are at war with the forces of evil, and Satan's strategy is to create conflict within the Christian camp. We easily fall for the devil's divisive and distracting tactics by becoming so preoccupied with examining our own spiritual belly buttons while the world perishes in sin around us. We too frequently major on the minors and minor with the majors."[5]

"For God so loved the world that He gave His only begotten Son, that whoever believes in Him should not perish but have everlasting life" (John 3:16, NKJV).

"Sin wounds. Sin mars. Sin disfigures. Sin destroys. And were it not for the cross of Calvary, sin's destruction would be permanent, irreversible. But God! How I love those words, 'But God.'"[6]

"My times are in thy hand" (Ps. 31:15).

"Therefore do not worry about tomorrow, for tomorrow will worry about its own things" (Matt. 6:34, NKJV).

"God does not waste pain and suffering. Instead, He uses it to mold us into the image of His Son and to teach us lessons we would probably learn no other way."[7]

"We beg for Your protection while the world seems

to fall apart around us. In the midst of the disaster we submit to You, we ask You to teach and perfect us through them. We plead for Your quick return. And while we wait on You, Lord, we will praise You. We will be joyful in You."[8]

"When life becomes especially hard and troubles seem to gang up on us, I have a few suggestions. . . . Ask the Lord to release your ingenuity, so that you can face the problem creatively with strength and wisdom. Remember that others experience troubles similar to yours. . . . God asks us to face these dead ends with an air of expectancy that his peace and power will prevail. And they will."[9]

"When a person embraces the Christian faith and says with assurance, 'I believe . . .,' then that person has truly embarked upon life."[10]

"God doesn't demand that we pray in King James English, or even with eloquence. Every feeble, stumbling prayer uttered by a believer is heard by God."[11]

THE JOURNALISTIC JOURNAL—YOUR TURN

Reserve a journal, or part of one, expressly for encouraging words written by authors you happen to "meet" in your reading. Read through these quotes as often as you need to for both spiritual and psychological battery recharges.

---

[1] Richard Foster, quoted in *Prayer Powerpoints,* comp. Randall D. Roth (Canada: Victor Books, 1995), p. 18.

[2] Andrew Murray, *The Ministry of Intercessory Prayer* (Minneapolis: Bethany House Publishers, 1981), p. 113.

[3] Tim Hansel, *You Gotta Keep Dancin',* quoted in *Hope in Times of Grief (Moving Through Sorrow),* comp. JoNancy Sundberg (Wheaton, Ill.: Harold Shaw Publishers, 1998), pp. 80, 81.

Write It on Your Heart

[4] Corrie ten Boom, *Clippings From My Notebook—Writings and Sayings Collected by Corrie ten Boom* (Minneapolis: World Wide Publications, 1982), p. 22.

[5] Doug Batchelor with Karen Liftshay, *How to Survive and Thrive in Church* (Sacramento, Calif.: Mountain Ministry, 1998), p. 120.

[6] Kay Arthur, *Lord, Heal My Hurts* (Sisters, Oreg.: Multnomah, 1989), p. 62.

[7] Marlene Bagnull, *Write His Answer* (Bloomington, Minn.: Bethany Press International, 1990, 1999), p. 57.

[8] Jeannie St. John Taylor, *Prayers for Troubled Times* (Chattanooga, Tenn.: AMG Publishers, 2002), p. 162.

[9] Barbara Johnson, quoted in *God Always Has a Plan B* (U.S.A.: Zondervan 1999), p. 11.

[10] R. C. Sproul, *Renewing Your Mind* (Grand Rapids: Baker Books, 1998), p. 13.

[11] Billy Graham, quoted in *Prayer Powerpoints,* p. 64.

Chapter 10

BLESS MOMMY AND DADDY

(The Prayer Request Journal)

*"And this is the confidence that we have in him, that,
if we ask any thing according to his will,
he heareth us: And if we know that he hear us,
whatsoever we ask, we know that we have
the petitions that we desired of him."*
—1 John 5:14, 15

WHAT IS A PRAYER REQUEST JOURNAL?

A Prayer Request Journal is one in which we can keep our special prayer requests.

The first prayer requests I remember laying before God were that He bless my mommy and daddy. Fifty-plus years later, however, I have so many people prayer concerns that I've had to divide them up between the seven days of the week.

One presenter at a Christian women's retreat confided that in order to keep her prayer lists from mushrooming until unmanageable, she periodically updates them, even removing names and situations if she feels God has brought healing or closure to them.

Beside individuals' names, I often annotate a specific request on their behalf. I do this because the experience of Bible characters shows us that God cares about the details in people's lives. For example, after asking that God prosper his plans (in general), Nehemiah prayed that God would grant him favor in the eyes of the king, for whom he worked (a specific) (Neh. 1:11).

The format of the Prayer Request Journal can be whatever you set it up to be. When I format a page for prayer requests, I make sure to leave enough space for the date on which I logged that particular request as well as a place to record updated information and answered prayers.

PRAYER REQUEST JOURNAL WRITING SAMPLE
"Monday's Prayer List"★

Date	Request	Status (Date)
1/11	Kids from church youth group	Mark raised grades (2/15)
		Sara broke up with Clint (4/11)
		Alan accepted Christ (5/13)
		Tommy suspended again (1/19)
6/28	Melinda and children	Melinda found a job! (9/2)
7/20	Bill and Suzanne Wenter	Still in good health at their age (8/4)
8/14	Phyllis Tillman	Diagnosed with lung cancer; looking for and praying about treatment options
9/17	Barbara	Struggling with unwanted divorce
9/21	Brigitte	Diagnosed with fast-

Date	Request	Status (Date)
		moving macular degeneration; depressed
9/25	The Balukus	Immigration papers for son came through! PTL! (3/17)
10/3	Charles	Back in jail; wants off drugs (12/5)
11/7	The Bartholomews	Marriage problems

Dear Father,

I pray Ephesians 1:16-19 over the people and the situations represented on today's prayer request list. I ask that You, the Father of glory, will give them the spirit of wisdom and a deeper knowledge of Yourself. I pray that You will open the eyes of their understanding so that they can understand that You are their hope in every situation. Their greatest inheritance is Your working in their behalf.

Thank You, Lord, for keeping these precious individuals in the shelter of Your hands today. In the name of Your Son I pray. Amen.

PRAYER REQUEST JOURNAL—YOUR TURN

Take a few minutes to write down three current prayer requests and today's date. Leave at least two lines between each request so that you have space to update the status of these requests.

★ Not real names or exact situations.

Chapter 11

ARMED TO THE TEETH

(The Spiritual Warfare Journal)

*"Put on the whole armour of God,
that ye may be able to stand against the wiles of the devil."*
—Eph. 6:11

WHAT IS A SPIRITUAL WARFARE JOURNAL?

A Spiritual Warfare Journal is very similar to a Prayer Request Journal. The only difference is that this journal has—in addition to an entry date and specific request—an annotated Bible promise to claim on behalf of each prayer concern. In fact, you can turn a Prayer Request Journal into a Spiritual Warfare Journal by simply adding promises.

Armin Gesswein states, "God's Word is known at the throne. Use it every time you pray. It is your prayer language." This is the language that helps wrest individuals and situations from the domain of the enemy. Praying God's Word back to Him also helps me keep focused when praying for people and situations.

I believe that praying in this manner adds spiritual effectiveness to our prayers because we are being biblical when we do so. After all, God has said, "Taste and see that I am good." "Prove Me." "Trust Me."

An added benefit of the Spiritual Warfare Journal is that repeating (on behalf of others) these promises on a regular basis helps us commit these scriptural principles (as well as their sources) to memory.

The format of the Spiritual Warfare Journal is similar to that of the Prayer Request Journal except enough space is allotted for Bible texts to be noted.

THE SPIRITUAL WARFARE JOURNAL WRITING SAMPLE

Here's what part of the page from the previous chapter's Prayer Request Journal request might look like as a Spiritual Warfare Journal.

"Monday's Spiritual Warfare List"

Date	Request	Status (Date)
1/11	Kids from church youth group *"I will save thy children" (Isa. 49:25). "Thy children shall be taught of the Lord" Isa. 54:13).*	Mark raised grades (2/15) Sara broke up with Clint (4/11) Alan accepted Christ (5/13) Tommy suspended again (1/19)
6/28	Melinda and children <u>Reminder to self:</u> Help widows, single parents, and fatherless *(see James 1:27).*	Melinda found a job! (9/2)
7/20	Bill and Suzanne Wenter *"They will still bear*	Still in good health at their age (8/4)

Date	Request	Status (Date)
	fruit in old age" *(Ps. 92:14, NIV).*	
8/14	Phyllis Tillman *"The Lord will* *strengthen [her]* *on her bed of illness;* *You will sustain [her]* *on [her] sickbed"* *(Ps. 41:3, NKJV).*	Diagnosed with lung cancer; looking for and praying about treatment options
9/17	Barbara *"For thy Maker is thine* *husband. . . . For the* *Lord hath called thee* *as a woman forsaken and* *grieved in spirit"* *(Isa. 54:5, 6).*	Struggling with un- wanted divorce
9/21	Brigitte *"And I will bring the* *blind by a way that* *they knew not; I will* *lead them in paths that* *they have not known:* *I will make darkness light* *before them, and crooked* *things straight. These things* *will I do unto them, and* *not forsake them" (Isa. 42:16).*	Diagnosed with fast- moving macular degeneration; depressed

Write It on Your Heart

THE SPIRITUAL WARFARE JOURNAL—YOUR TURN

Consider transforming your Prayer Request Journal into a Spiritual Warfare Journal by jotting down an appropriate text or promise below each entry.*

---

* You can readily find relevant texts in a Bible concordance. Also, a number of inexpensive Bible promise books are currently on the market.

Chapter 12

HOW CAN I GET MORE _____?

(The Needful Subjects Journal)

"And thine ears shall hear a word behind thee, saying,
This is the way, walk ye in it."
—Isa. 30:21

WHAT IS A NEEDFUL SUBJECTS JOURNAL?

The Needful Subjects Journal is a journal (or a section of one) in which you jot down Bible texts, quotes, and new insights you have concerning areas of interest and/or need in your life.

For example, you may desire to know more about a specific doctrine, how to pray more effectively, or how to discover God's will for a decision you need to make.

I've been amazed at how God speaks to my innermost personal needs almost *anywhere* I turn in the Bible for devotional reading. For example, here is what I found in a superficial skimming of three random chapters.

a. From the *Old Testament:* Psalm 103 addresses issues of fear, children, health, guilt, pain of the past, anger, low self-esteem, who God is, obedience, and trust.

b. From the *New Testament:* Luke 4 deals with how to overcome any kind of temptation, how and when to keep the Sabbath, our duty to others, faith, spiritual warfare, the power of Christ, and balance in personal ministry.

c. A random chapter from the book of Proverbs (Proverbs 14) addresses the following: how to be a wise woman, how to choose one's words, integrity of action and speech, a critical tongue, laughing at sin [think about the content of most sitcoms], heavy hearts, controlling anger, relationship with our neighbors, planning good things for others, how to cooperate with God in order to have safe sanctuary, politicians, envying others, and how to avoid looking stupid in public!

During my single years a needful subject in my life was how to know God's will concerning my marital status. More specifically, I wanted to know God's will concerning a certain gentleman friend who had surfaced among my acquaintances into my single-for-life world.

Over a period of about two years—mostly during my morning devotions—God revealed His will to me, little by little. At the same time He also revealed some heartwork I needed to do before I could clearly discern whether or not to accept a marriage proposal should it come my way. Since God's timing is perfect, the marriage proposal came soon *after* I knew God's answer—again, mostly from my personal Bible study and ongoing journal notes.

The writing style of the Needful Subjects Journal is whatever works for you. Personally, I like to keep a separate page for each of my needful subjects so that I have plenty of room to add thoughts and Bible texts as they turn up.

THE NEEDFUL SUBJECTS JOURNAL WRITING SAMPLES

SAMPLE 1: "HOLINESS"

One of my felt subjects of need: *Claimable Promises for Holiness in an Unholy World*

- "I pray not that thou shouldest take them out of the world, but that thou shouldst keep them from the evil" (John 17:15).

- "But as he which hath called you is holy, so be ye holy in all manner of conversation; because it is written, Be ye holy; for I am holy" (1 Peter 1:15, 16).

- "I beseech you . . . by the mercies of God that ye present your bodies a living sacrifice, holy, acceptable unto God. . . . Be ye transformed by the renewing of your mind, that ye may prove what is that good, and acceptable, and perfect, will of God" (Rom. 12:1, 2).

- "What manner of persons ought ye to be in all holy conversation and godliness, looking for and hasting unto the coming of the day of God" (2 Peter 3:11, 12).

- "And may the Lord make you increase and abound in love to one another and to all, just as we do to you, so that He may establish your hearts blameless in holiness before our God and Father at the coming of our Lord Jesus Christ with all His saints" (1 Thess. 3:12, 13, NKJV). (I love how this final passage implies that growing in holiness is also growing in love.)

SAMPLE 2: "ASSORTED THOUGHTS ON FEAR"
(PARAPHRASED)

- The fearless are those who keep their minds on the workings and way of God (Ps. 119:23).
- God promises relief from fear (Prov. 1:33).
- Our exchanging trust in God for fear of human-made situations brings us into the safety of God's care (Prov. 29:25).
- If we've asked God to be with us, we are not to worry about what others can do to us (Ps. 118:6).
- Needlessly fearing something can bring it upon us (Prov. 10:24).
- God is not the one who makes us afraid (2 Tim. 1:7).

I'm amazed by all the times in the Bible that God told people to "fear not!" "Fear not" seemed to be His special words to comfort His children in times of distress, terror, and confusion.

- God to Moses (Num. 21:34).
- God to Joshua (Joshua 8:1).
- God to Israel (Isa. 43:5).
- God to Daniel (Dan. 10:19).
- Jesus to His hearers, including us (Matt. 10:31; Luke 12:32).
- Christ to John the revelator (Rev. 1:17).
- Christ to the persecuted (Rev. 2:10).

NEEDFUL SUBJECTS JOURNAL—YOUR TURN

1. Identify at least three issues/needs/questions you have right now (for example, loneliness, shaky faith, poor family relations, fear of totally trusting God, life after

death, a certain life habit, a decision you need to make).

2. Identify each of your chosen subjects on three different stickies. Using the stickies as page markers. At the top of each stickie-tabulated page, write down a needful subject.

3. Before your devotional/journal time each day, thank God for specific blessings, confess specific sins, and then ask Him—as You are reading His Word—to direct your mind to helpful information in each of your needful areas.

4. As you come across texts that give you information on these subjects, jot them down on the appropriate page. Over time, watch for life-guiding principles that will emerge as you continue writing in your Needful Subjects Journal pages.* Then, in God's timing and as He prepares the way, act on these principles.

This type of journaling can lead to a precious and practical walk with Christ.

---

* Take care, however, not to base a major decision on just one or two texts. Also, be sure to take into consideration the context of each quote (no doubt, you've heard the saying "A text without a context is a pretext").

Chapter 13

WRITE IT ON MY HEART

(The Scripture Memorization Journal)

*"Thy word have I hid in mine heart,
that I might not sin against thee."*
—Ps. 119:11

WHAT IS A SCRIPTURE MEMORIZATION JOURNAL?

The Scripture Memorization Journal is a journal—or a journal section—in which you copy down Bible passages you want to memorize. I believe that, given the times in which we live, this is perhaps the most important journal we could keep. I believe this for a number of reasons.

⍺ *Knowing Scripture from memory helps us fight off temptation.*

"Temptations often appear irresistible because, through neglect of prayer and the study of the Bible, the tempted one cannot readily remember God's promises and meet Satan with the Scripture weapons."[1]

⍺ *Knowing Scripture gives us moral, spiritual, and emotional courage.*

As never before, we need the divine strength that comes from meditating upon God's memorized Word. We need the promises of Psalm 91 committed to heart, to keep us in the secret place of the Most High.

We need to know that "God is our refuge and strength, a very present help in trouble. Therefore will not we fear, though the earth [under the foundations of lower Manhattan even] be removed, and though the mountains be carried into the midst of the sea."[2]

In an era of terror and war, we need to be able to say, as did Paul, "none of these things move me, neither count I my life dear unto myself, so that I might finish my course with joy."[3]

    Only the knowledge and power of God's Word will enable responses of courage and guide our feet through the complex end-time prophetic events we see so quickly unfolding even on our television screens.

A Scripture Memorization Journal keeps us in touch with what we believe and why. Some people I know have transferred their journal entries onto 3 x 5 cards for quick pocket or purse retrieval before heading out for the day. That way they can avoid wasting time during a doctor's office wait or even at a long stoplight.

The format of a Scripture Memorization Journal is whatever benefits the journal keeper.

THE SCRIPTURE MEMORIZATION JOURNAL WRITING SAMPLE

Though originally noted in a Scripture Memorization Journal, I have since transferred the following texts to purse-sized, self-laminated cards for transport, easy access, and quick review. (Clear adhesive plastic shelf "paper" works well for a grass-roots lamination job.)

    Psalm 91

    John 14

- Psalms 15, 23, and 121
- Lamentations 3:20-24
- Hebrews 4:12, 14-16; 7:25-27

Somewhere along the line, I also annotated the following quotes as reminders concerning the importance of consistent Scripture memorization.

"We are to come before the mercy seat with reverence, calling up to our mind the promises that God has given. . . . We are not to trust in our finite prayers, but in the word of our heavenly Father, in His assurance of His love for us." [4]

"Keep your Bible with you. As you have opportunity, read it; fix the texts in your memory. Even while you are walking the streets you may read a passage and meditate upon it, thus fixing it in mind. . . .

"By Bible study and daily communion with Jesus we shall gain clear, well-defined views of individual responsibility and strength to stand in the day of trial and temptation. He whose life is united to Christ by hidden links will be kept by the power of God through faith unto salvation." [5]

Have you ever thought about carrying a little purse-sized Bible with you or keeping one in your car? Most religious bookstores carry a number of pocket-sized, inexpensive, and lightweight New Testaments and even entire Bibles. (My slim electronic Bible takes up less purse space than my electronic personal calendar. It even has a function for "bookmarking" passages I'm memorizing.)

"Their [believers'] preparation is to be made day by day, in treasuring up in their hearts the precious truths of God's word, in feeding upon the teaching of Christ, and through prayer strengthening their faith; then, when brought into trial, the Holy Spirit will bring to their re-membrance the very truths that will reach the hearts of those who shall come to hear.

"God will flash the knowledge obtained by diligent searching of the Scriptures, into their memory at the very time when it is needed"[6]

Memorizing Scripture also prepares us to share with others. Peter counsels us to "sanctify the Lord God in your hearts: and be ready always to give an answer to every man that asketh you a reason of the hope that is in you with meekness and fear" (1 Peter 3:15).

THE SCRIPTURE MEMORIZATION JOURNAL— YOUR TURN

Before you go to bed this evening, choose a text to memorize this week.

Set up a personal memorization program.

Ask God to direct you to the portions of Scripture you personally will need to carry you through tough times. And then go for it.

Remember, Christ's knowledge of the Scriptures is how He avoided being deceived during His wilderness temptations and gained victory over the enemy.

---

[1] Ellen G. White, *The Great Controversy,* p. 600.

[2] Ps. 46:1, 2.

[3] Acts 20:24.

[4] Ellen G. White, *In Heavenly Places,* p. 125.

[5] *Ibid.,* p. 138.

[6] Ellen G. White, *Counsels on Sabbath School Work,* pp. 40, 41.

Chapter 14

POTPOURRI

(The Mix-and-Match Devotional Journal)

"Oh, that the Almighty would answer me,
That my Prosecutor had written a book!"
—Job[1]

"Potpourri: . . . a miscellaneous anthology or collection."[2]

WHAT IS A POTPOURRI JOURNAL?

Perhaps you, like me, love walking through the home decorating section of a department store. I can smell the fragrance of potpourri packages long before I get to the aisle where they are displayed. Ah, aromas of vanilla, dusty rose, gardenia, tangerine, rosewood . . .

Each package, whatever the scent, contains a variety of plant parts—everything from dried rose petals and evergreen sprigs to tiny pinecones. Yet each miscellaneous item in the same package, no matter how it differs from the rest of the contents, still carries the same aromatic fragrance.

Likewise, a *Mix-and-Match Devotional Journal* is whatever combination of journaling styles you want to use—mixed and matched inside the same cover. The styles may differ, but each varied section in this journal still emits the fragrance of God's love at work in your life.

You design a Potpourri Journal to meet your current

needs. You adapt and modify it as your needs and circumstances change.

Several years ago, after I finished presenting a seminar on journaling to secondary students in Palau, one of the young men asked to speak with me. Shyly he produced a prayer journal. His was a true Potpourri Journal—with one big difference. He had not divided it into sections—everything (prayer requests, praises, copied texts) just appeared to be "dumped" into this journal without any forethought.

However, it worked beautifully for him . . . because he was an artist!

In amazement, I looked at the clean, original artwork this gifted young man had incorporated into his journal. Simple praying hands graced the beginning of each prayer request. A flaming sword (à la Hebrews 4:12) indicated instructive scriptural passages he had copied. A broken heart indicated changes he felt God was calling him to make. A simple 3-D cross identified references specific to Christ. This journal was an original work of art!

Maybe you too are artistic . . . or you scrapbook . . . or stamp . . . or do calligraphy. Don't hesitate to enhance and embellish your journals with your own creative touches!

The format of a Mix-and-Match Devotional Journal will be whatever your needs dictate.

MIX-AND-MATCH DEVOTIONAL JOURNAL—YOUR TURN
Just do it!

---

[1] Job 31:35, NKJV.

[2] *The American Heritage Dictionary,* 2nd college ed. (Boston: Houghton Mifflin Company, 1985), p. 970.

Chapter 15

THE FINAL WORD

*"'Write out of your life experiences,' He [God] said to me.
'Make yourself transparent and vulnerable so others can see
what I have done, and am doing, in your life.'"*
—**Marlene Bagnulli**★

Journaling brings its own rewards. The blessings and insights that come from journaling are different for every journal keeper.

Remember that stack of old letters my mother had saved? The Family Heirloom Journal into which these letters evolved became my son's favorite birthday gift on his thirty-third birthday. He will pore over this journal—and share the memories it evokes—for years to come.

You see, the journal I gave my son is not about the mechanics of writing, or even about the cute things he said and did during his "terrible twos." At its deepest level, the journal is really about a unique and precious relationship that he and I had at a certain period in our lives. Somewhere in the storage of our shop my husband, Jim, and I have two big boxes of cards and letters that we exchanged prior to, and then during, our engagement. Another box contains annotated cards and letters we've shared since we got married six years ago.

In addition to all of the above, Jim and I continually

keep each other's most recent annotated cards on our respective dressers and desks. The little notes we've jotted down on these cards comprise an ongoing "journal" of our relationship. Going through them and sharing them anew revives memories of our premarriage and marital milestones.

Likewise, the journaling you and I do also keeps fresh in our minds the people and events that have shaped us. More important, however, journaling often chronicles a growing relationship with—and an increasing understanding of—the God who created and sustained us during the twists and turns of our journeys.

If you have acted on the journaling suggestions in the preceding chapters, you have already created a customized journal sampler between the covers of this very book. Along the way you, no doubt, identified at least one type of journaling that would truly meet a current need in your life, whether that be enhanced personal devotional time or an encouragement ministry to someone else.

DON'T WORRY

Don't worry if journaling doesn't meet your spiritual needs *every single* day. My primary journal (a Potpourri Journal) I pull from the bookcase no more than three times a week during my morning devotional time. Once a week I use another one for notes and insights during Tuesday night group Bible study.

I write in a third journal about twice a month—on those rare occasions when I find time to continue reading through an old, yet fascinating, book about Christ's life. In this journal I note points that apply to my current spiritual walk.

Since I was diagnosed with cancer some time back, I

have begun a new journal—a Collections Journal. In this quickly expanding notebook I keep comforting and encouraging comments (whether handwritten or by e-mail) from friends who are prayerfully supporting me through my treatment.

Journals have a way of becoming part of our personal support systems through tough times. They can help carry us through a personal crisis. They can become an auxiliary road map for this season of life. Yet I can't emphasize enough the ministry potential of a journal.

A few years ago, when I'd finished presenting at a convocation in a northern state, a young woman asked to speak with me in private. When we were alone she reached into her handbag and pulled out a small, beige three-ring binder, which she handed me.

Shyly she said, "The Lord impressed me to make this for you."

I slowly thumbed through the 3 x 5 cards in this little binder, each one in her handwriting, bearing an encouraging text or inspirational quote (a veritable Collection Journal).

The young woman continued, "I've had some terribly hard times in my life. I began a little encouragement journal for myself, one I could carry in my purse. I know you've been through a lot of hard times too, so I copied down my journal quotes to share with you. I hope they help."

Her hope has been *more* than realized. I can't tell you what a precious gift this journal from a total stranger has become to me! I too have carried it in my purse. I too have read its precious promises to my husband on dark days. I have even copied a number of the quotes and passed them on to friends struggling through the aftermath of personal tragedy.

My mother was so right when she said, "A journal is a gift that keeps on giving."

Before we end our time together in this book, I want you to start thinking "outside the box," as the expression goes, when it comes to your journal entries.

As you creatively and prayerfully journal, be on the lookout for thoughts and anecdotes that you *(yes, you!)* could develop into the following speaking and writing opportunities:

- A children's story that *you* could tell in one of the children's classes of your church
- A children's story that *you* could share during the children's spot of your church's worship service
- A special feature that *you* could share during your church's adult study time (Go ahead and volunteer—program superintendents are *always* looking for fresh, new special features. God has been at work in *your* life, so why *not* you?)
- A devotional article in a monthly or bimonthly publication that features daily devotionals, such as *The Upper Room*. (Request the guidelines before submitting your devotional!)
- A stand-alone devotional that you could submit for inclusion in any number of annual women's devotional books (You can *do* it—just write for the publishing companies' guidelines!)
- An article (based on one of your journal entries) in a Christian women's magazine (Once again, write for the guidelines!)
- Your *own* book of devotionals (Don't laugh!

Where do you think much of the raw material for my books originated? Right . . . in my journals!)

Do you want to encourage others?

Do you want to comfort them?

Do you want to serve and witness for your Lord?

Then remember that one of the most effective methods for all of the above is simply sharing with others what God has done for you personally. This was Christ's command to the healed demoniac: "Tell what great things God has done for you" (Luke 8:39, NKJV).

Sara, tell someone else how God brought you through that unexpected divorce!

Kashina, pass on what God taught you, even though you didn't get the job you wanted!

Pearl, share how God sustained you through the loss of your son!

Niki, refresh our hearts with your special miracle story!

Debra, show us how God stuck by you, even through your poor choices, when everybody else gave up on you!

When you share what God has done for *you*, you rewrite God's caring love on *your* heart. When other hearts meet yours and read what you—and He—have written there, He, through you, encourages them and draws them closer to Himself.

Don't you love the idea of being one of God's Potpourri Journals? I do!

I also love thinking about the final journal entries at the end of time, which He has promised to write on your heart and mine.

Can't you just see Christ picking up that glorious white feathery plume and dipping it in a crystalline bottle of light, pulsating with intermittent rainbow hues?

Oh, the thrill of anticipation as we stand before Him! With bated breath, we watch as He brings the glistening point of His eternal pen toward each heart and writes the entry He promised, so long ago, to write on the hearts of overcomers.

"I will write on him [you and me] the name of My God and the name of the city of My God, the New Jerusalem, which comes down out of heaven from My God. And I will write on him My new name" (Rev. 3:12, NKJV).

Imagine! Throughout eternity, we will joyfully bear—before the universe—the name and signature of the Author and Finisher of our faith (Heb. 12:2)!

I want to meet you up there. I want to compare journal entries. How about it—is it a date? Wonderful!

So until then, what I say to you, I also say to myself.

Write! Write His love on your heart—so that you won't forget.

Let Him shower you with the special blessings that come from recording His love in one-of-a-kind journals that only *you* can keep.

Let Him lead you to profound communion with Him—and minister to other hurting hearts through *your* words and life experiences.

Let Him have His way with you so that *His* heart can find the most personal, fulfilling, and joyful relationship it's ever had . . . with *yours!*

YOUR TURN

Dear Father,

Thank You that no page of my life is too small, too

tattered, too torn, or too smudged for You to write upon.

Thank You for the gifts of prayer and the Word, through which the heavenly Journal Keeper communicates with me.

Show me more specifically how to internalize Your love and then share it with others in unique and creative ways. Show me how to become Your journal.

I praise You for your consistent care and thank You for leading me in exciting new directions as You and I both continue the heartwork of writing.

In Your precious name I pray.

Amen.

---

* Marlene Bagnull, *Write His Answer* (Bloomington, Minn.: Bethany Press International, 1999), p. 16.